He was to marry a young woman named Mary.

One day, an angel swept
down from the sky. "Do not
be afraid," he said to Mary.
"You are going to
have a baby."

"He will be the Son of
God and his name
will be Jesus."

Trembling, Mary knelt before the angel.
"I am God's servant," she replied.
"I will do as he wishes."

When Joseph heard the news, he was deeply puzzled.
That night, he dreamed of an angel.
"Mary is having God's son," the angel told him.

Soon after, Mary and Joseph were married.
"I'll take care of you and the baby," Joseph promised.
But then a messenger from King Herod arrived.

"Everyone has to return to the place where they
were born, to pay a special tax," he declared.

Joseph and Mary had to travel to Bethlehem,
many miles away. Together, they set off...

...over the green hills
of Galilee, all the way
to Bethlehem.

They arrived in the starry dark. As they wandered the sleeping streets, Joseph knocked on door after door.

No room here!

Everywhere the answer was the same. "We're full!" the innkeepers declared.

At the very last inn, the innkeeper shook his head. "I can only offer you a place in my stable," he said.

Joseph made Mary a bed out of straw and
she lay down, weary from her journey.
That night, her baby was born.

Mary wrapped him in a swaddling cloth.
With no cradle for his bed, she laid him
gently in a manger, lined with hay.

On the hills outside Bethlehem, drowsy
shepherds were watching their sheep.

A glowing angel appeared before them.
"Hurry to Bethlehem!" he said.
"There you will find a baby in a
manger. He is the Son of God."

At once, the sky was bright with angels.

"Glory to God," they sang.

"Peace on earth and goodwill to all men."

The shepherds rushed to the stable and
knelt before the baby Jesus, filled with joy.

When they told Mary what the
angels had said, she looked
at her baby in wonder.

She treasured their
words in her heart.

Far away in the east,
some wise men saw
a shining star.

"It's a sign," they cried.
"A new King has
been born tonight."

For many days and nights, they
rode across the desert, following
the shining star. At last, they came
to the little town of Bethlehem.

The star hovered over a tumbledown stable, and they went inside.

Kneeling down, the wise men worshipped the baby.

"We have brought gifts for the newborn King," they said, opening caskets of...

gold...

frankincense...

and myrrh.

Then God appeared to Joseph in a dream. "You must leave at once," He said. "Your child is in danger from King Herod."

The journey home was
long and hard, but Mary
and Joseph had hope
in their hearts.

They knew their child would grow
up to do great and wonderful things.

The story of baby Jesus is over two thousand years old. It comes
from the section of the Bible known as the New Testament,
in the parts written by Saint Luke and Saint Matthew.

Edited by Lesley Sims

Designed by Samantha Barrett

First published in 2014 by Usborne Publishing Ltd., Usborne House, 83-85 Saffron Hill, London EC1N 8RT, England.
www.usborne.com   Copyright © 2014 Usborne Publishing Ltd.